The Great Dune Buggy Race

Meet Leap's Friends

Della

Tim

Grandpa

Leap

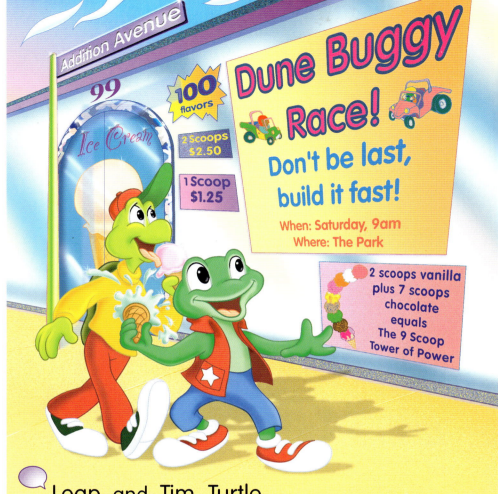

Leap and Tim Turtle were getting ice cream when they saw it — an eye-popping, tongue-stopping, cone-dropping announcement!

"Are you thinking what I'm thinking?" asked Leap.

"To Grandpa's shop we go!" yelled Tim.

💬 They found Grandpa waiting for them with sketches and plans. "We've got a **buggy to build!**" he said. "I've got a **list** of everything you'll need right over…now where did I put that?"

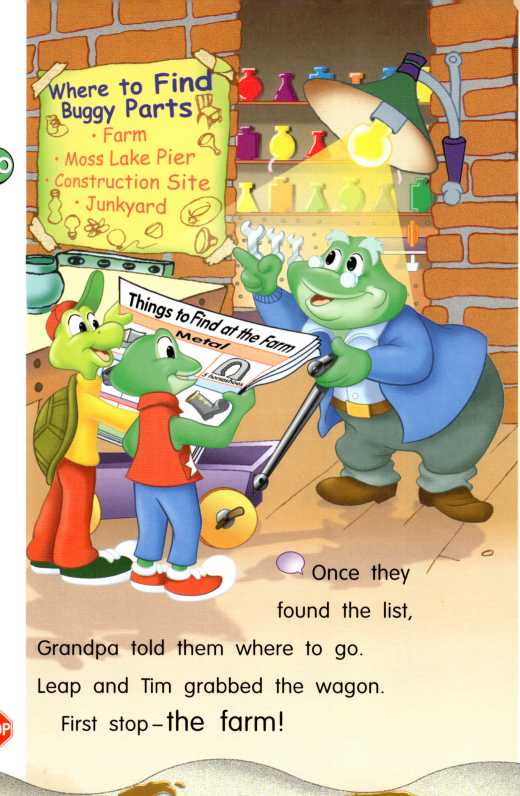

Once they found the list, Grandpa told them where to go. Leap and Tim grabbed the wagon. First stop—the farm!

The farmer was thrilled to see them. "Help!" he cried. "My prized chickens!" The chickens had flown the coop. Leap and Tim rushed over to help.

 When the coop was full of chickens and the hay was chicken-free, Leap and Tim collected the buggy parts on **the list**.

"Y'all take anything you need!" said the farmer.
"Yee haw!"

Things to Find at the Farm

Metal
- 1 anvil
- 4 spikes
- 5 horseshoes

Rubber
- 1 tire
- 1 inner tube
- 2 boots

Plastic
- 1 bucket
- 1 doll
- 2 soda bottles

Glass
- 2 vases
- 1 window
- 5 light bulbs

Next stop – the beach, and boy, was it hot!

Tim and Leap were about to search the beach for dune buggy parts when they saw their friend Della Duck. She was swamped. "Leap! Tim!" she yelled. "Help!"

 Her lemonade stand was jumping, but her customers were cranky.

"Sugar-free lemonade, no ice!" yelled one.

"Double-lemon lemonade to go!" yelled another.

After Della, Leap, and Tim had finished serving every last customer, they combed the beach for more buggy parts.

Nothing was safe from the three buggy-teers! Then they headed to the construction site.

Things to Find at Moss Lake Pier

Metal
- 1 lunch box
- 3 propellers
- 5 license plates

Rubber
- 1 tire
- 5 balloons
- 4 flip flops

Plastic
- 1 toy bucket
- 1 toy shovel
- 2 beach balls

Glass
- 1 mirror
- 5 bottles
- 1 ship porthole

The construction foreman was waiting in front of a very big woodpile.

"Finally! You're here!" he hollered when he saw them.

"Excuse me?" said Leap.

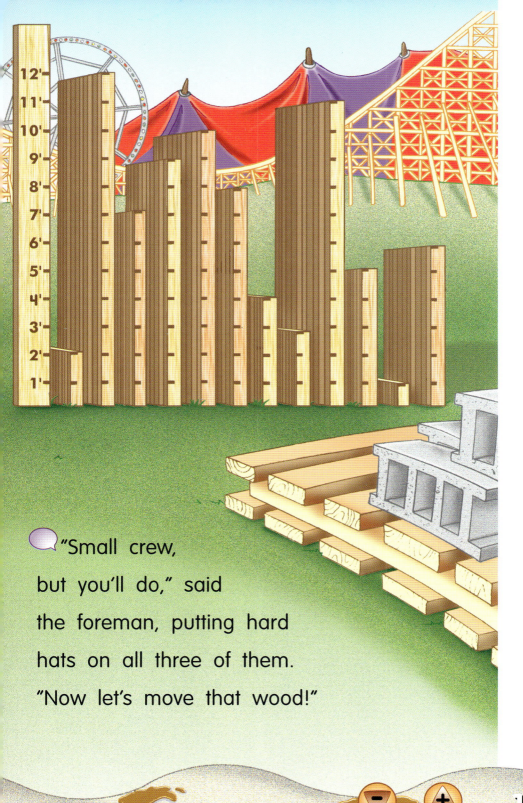

"Small crew, but you'll do," said the foreman, putting hard hats on all three of them. "Now let's move that wood!"

When they were finished, there was no time to rest.

"There are buggy parts and more here," said the foreman. "So hop to it!"

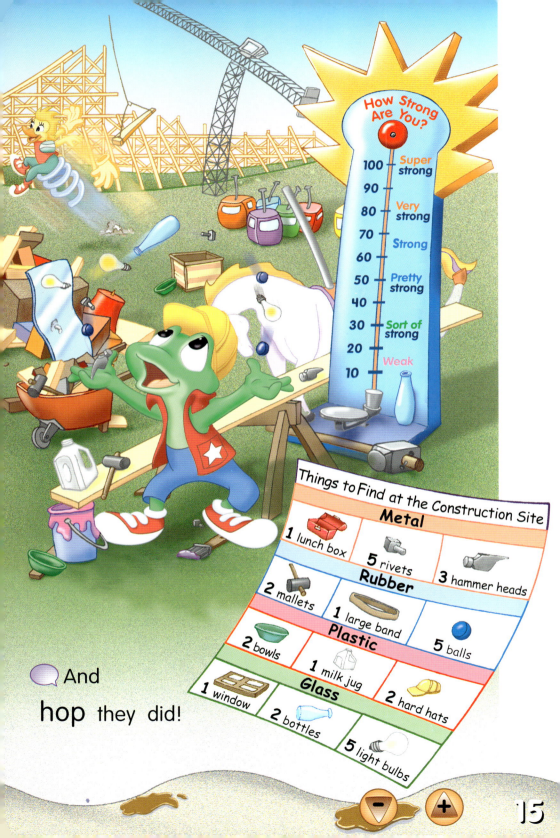

Last stop – the junkyard!

"We'll find lots of cool stuff here!" yelled Tim.

"That's right," said the junkyard man. "Just as soon as you help me CRUSH SOME CARS!"

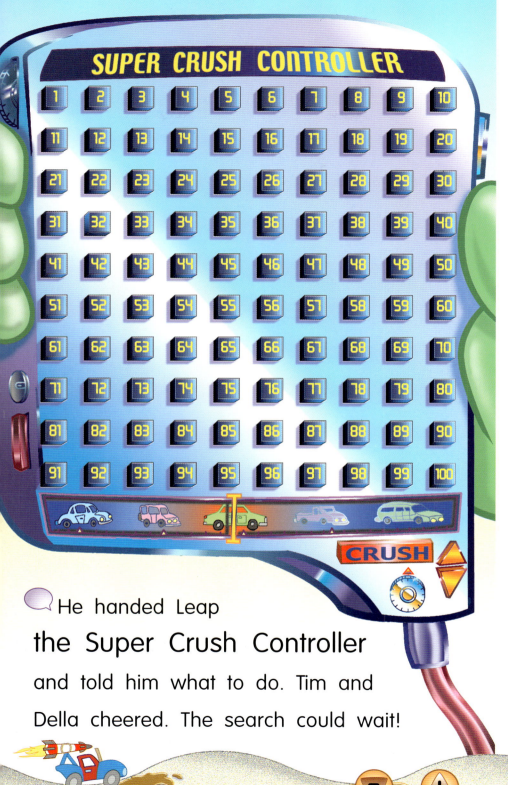

💬 He handed Leap the Super Crush Controller and told him what to do. Tim and Della cheered. The search could wait!

After a car-crunching, scrap-munching good time, they loaded more parts into the wagon.

Suddenly, something caught Leap's eye. He saw an old model rocket!

"That's it!" he cried. "Just what I need to make the buggy go extra fast. Now I'm sure to win!"

Things to Find at the Junkyard

Metal
- 4 hub caps
- 4 springs
- 2 car doors

Rubber
- 1 hose
- 3 tires
- 3 inner tubes

Plastic
- 1 helmet
- 2 chairs

Glass
- 3 bottles
- 2 plates
- 3 soda bottles
- 2 head lights

When Grandpa saw all the parts they had collected, he was very excited. The three friends put the parts into Grandpa's dune buggy machine, and crossed their fingers.

💬 The machine sputtered and whirred. It hiccupped and spit out...the fastest, scrappiest, snappiest dune buggy ever!

Leap hopped into the driver's seat. "This is awesome!"

The day of the race Leap waited nervously. He would have to be super fast to win.

"On your marks, get set..."

"Go Leap!" yelled the crowd.
Leap's buggy zipped around the course!

Leap crossed the finish line and looked up at the clock. The crowd roared.
LEAP HAD WON!